Basic Operations: ESTATE PLANNING for Business Owners

THE RIGHT ATTORNEY CAN PROTECT
YOUR BUSINESS AND FAMILY'S FUTURE

Attorney A.J. Yolofsky

Jacobs & Whitehall
21750 Hardy Oak Blvd
Suite 104
#51700
San Antonio, Texas 78258
www.jacobsandwhitehall.com

Ordering Information:

Quantity sales. Special discounts are available on quantity purchases by corporations, associations, and others. For details, contact the publisher at the address above.

Orders by U.S. trade bookstores and wholesalers. Please contact Jacobs & Whitehall: Tel: (888) 991-2766 or visit www.jacobsandwhitehall.com.

Printed in the United States of America

Published in 2022

ISBN: 978-1-954506-56-5

Dedication

This book is for the doers, the risk-takers, the people who know the sometimes lonely journey of building something from nothing. It's the entrepreneur who takes the chance to change their own life, which sometimes leads to changing the lives of other people, especially their families and loved ones.

This book is to help them preserve their legacy.

DISCLAIMER

This publication is intended to be used for educational purposes only. No legal advice is being given, and no attorney-client relationship is intended to be created by reading this material. The author assumes no liability for any errors or omissions or for how this book or its contents are used or interpreted, or for any consequences resulting directly or indirectly from the use of this book. For legal or any other advice, please consult an experienced attorney or the appropriate expert, who is aware of the specific facts of your case and is knowledgeable in the law in your jurisdiction.

Yolofsky Law
One Financial Plaza, Suite 1000,
Fort Lauderdale, FL 33394
(954) 237 4011
hello@yolofskylaw.com
www.yolofskylaw.com

TESTIMONIALS

"Attorney Yolofsky offers exceptional service to his clients with detailed explanations and a unique insight helping to ease nerves and focus on the legal issues at hand. As an attorney myself, I was beyond impressed with his approach. I reached out to him when I had a legal issue present itself that I knew nothing about. He took the time to talk me through each legal issue, explaining to me the pros and cons and ultimately advising me on the best next steps. Truthfully, being on the non-attorney side even as an attorney is nerve-wracking. He not only gave me confidence but he reassured me that he would be there step by step if necessary. He truly cares about his clients. And I have definitely learned quite a few things for my own practice from him. 5 stars isn't enough for how exceptional he truly is! Thank you so much!"

– Samantha Allen

****

"If you are looking for a thoughtful, sharp, creative, and professional attorney to handle your estate and business planning matters, you have found your guy. A.J. consistently uses his top-notch analytical and legal skills to help navigate tricky situations and develop a plan of action. I could not recommend him more to anyone who wants to know they have a trusted advisor who is looking after their needs with the utmost care and attention."

– Alanna Pearl

****

"Making the decision to hire A.J. has been one of the best decisions for my husband and me when it comes to our businesses. He not only helps us lay the foundation but helps us with protecting our and our family's future. Because of his background as a Marine Corps Officer, A.J.'s approach is very different, and might I add, he thinks outside of the box which is what we appreciate about him. He is a strategist, and that is what sets him apart from the rest. He is always willing and available to speak with us, answer any questions that we may have, and is always there for us when we need his guidance before we make a decision. A.J. is the best lawyer to have in your corner because he will go above and beyond to deliver what is best for you, your business, and your family. A.J. Yolofsky emulates "a hero to your family, a hero to your business."

– Deanna Knowles

****

"A.J. is a very competent lawyer. I would like to highlight two more characteristics: empathic and ethical. In my company, we are very comfortable working with his law firm and we have the certainty that our interests are very well represented by him."

– Paolo Longo

****

"A.J. has the extraordinary skillset of intelligence, legal knowledge, business sense, and an uncanny foresight in planning. He is genuinely dedicated to the care of his clients and their future. I recommend him without hesitation."

– Michael McDonald

****

"A.J. is a straight shooter. He is very knowledgeable, and he uses this knowledge and expertise to help me. He has helped my business a lot, and I'm always thrilled to refer him to any of my friends. He's a good man and an excellent lawyer, and he has a skilled team with him. I trust him and his crew."

– Robert Hernandez

****

TABLE OF CONTENTS

About The Author

Eighteen years ago, I started practicing law as a commercial litigator after years of service as a strategist in the U.S. Marine Corps.

Over the course of my legal career, I have worked in nearly every kind of law firm – from boutique practices to international partnerships – and I have handled cases both big and small.

Whether counseling condominium residents in cases regarding the width of a parking lot or representing an Iraqi construction company in international arbitration over the construction of an army base; I've seen it all.

But no matter the size of my firm or the scope of my client's legal issues, I focus on each client as if they are the sole mission by bringing strategic planning and a commitment to success that is unmatched by other attorneys.

My Story Begins Here

As a commercial litigation attorney, I worked constantly. I handled countless cases across the country, and across the world.

But everything changed for me in 2016 when my wife was diagnosed with stage III breast cancer.

The disease was extremely aggressive and she started treatment immediately. Shortly after her diagnosis, she went into surgery - and I found myself in a hospital waiting room thinking about the time we'd spent together in our marriage.

As I reflected on all my memories with her, something started to become painfully clear to me. I realized that my life as a commercial litigator had put me in a position where I wasn't in control of my time.

My personal life was constantly subject to the schedules of opposing counsel, tied up in court deadlines across the U.S., and I was often working all hours of the day to accommodate time zones in other countries around the world.

There were so many different people taking my time – people who needed my services – but they took me away from the person who needed me most, and who I held most dear.

It was clear that I needed a change, but I had no idea what that change was going to be.

Over the next month, I spent a lot of time being everything but an attorney while my wife recovered from her surgery. It was a wake-up call that helped me understand how important it is to prioritize your own life and the people you love. So, in between the time I spent caring for her, I started researching what I could do to get control of my life back.

One day, I came across a program that explained how to find independence by maintaining a healthy work-life balance. I figured out that I wanted to open my own practice in an area of law that would allow me to really help people while still having time to be present in my own life.

This is what started the journey that brought me to estate planning.

I Found A New Path Forward

At first, my knowledge of estate planning was from some trust disputes and what I learned in law school, but I quickly realized that there are some universal benefits that would come from owning my own business.

First, (and most importantly), I would be able to find autonomy and get my life back. By running my own business, I would be the one to set my schedule and I could take on clients at a pace that allowed me to spend time with the people I love.

What's more, I found that estate planning is an area of law that helps people stay out of court by guiding them through the steps of prevention.

Second, I started to experience the difference in the quality of life that comes with investing in yourself.

Back in my days at larger firms, there were times I would work tirelessly on a case, knowing that I was making a difference – so I thought. There were some cases where I was just one more cog in a hundred-spoked wheel. By working for clients as my own boss, I wouldn't have to overwork myself to make a senior partner look good. Instead, I would be putting my client's needs first rather than racking up billable hours. In fact, I mostly did away with billable hours once I opened my own firm.

But the importance of self-investment didn't stop there. In fact, it went directly in hand with the work that I wanted to do: help people invest in their future, create a solid foundation, and gain peace of mind through estate and business planning.

Today, I have control over my life, I can invest in myself, and my career allows me to help people.

<u>I Personally Understand The Importance Of Estate Planning</u>

When I look back now, the road that took me to where I am today seems somewhat ironic.

When my wife got her cancer diagnosis, we were in our mid-40s, we had children, and we both worked hard with the hope that we could build a foundation of wealth for our family. But we didn't have any kind of plan for the crisis we were facing – no estate plan, no strategy . . .nothing.

The funny thing is, I had been an attorney for years at that point. If anyone was supposed to have an estate plan by now, it would be me.

This made me wonder: If my wife and I should have known all this and even we didn't take these important steps . . . who else is missing this mark? Who else is leaving the fruits of all their efforts vulnerable to the "what ifs" that may, one day, actually happen?

This question helped me realize something . . .

Other People Needed Estate Planning . . . And I Could Help Them Do It

Families like mine need this work, and they need someone who can help guide them through the process. Not only could this be a great business opportunity, but I could also really help people. Years of litigation practice showed me how businesses and people could have avoided court altogether if they had spent a little more time working on their plans.

Too many business owners, (and often small business owners in particular), are so busy building their business that they have little time to think about how to prepare a contingency plan.

While building something valuable to offer your community is important in and of itself, it's easy to forget how crucial it is to have a strong foundation. You want a house, not a house of cards.

So I Changed My Direction

In 2016, I shifted the focus of my corporate practice, and over the next six months, I put myself through extensive estate planning training.

I had done some trust and probate litigation over the years — but I knew that wasn't going to cut it.

I did three full cycles worth of continuing legal education in that time - equaling about three years' worth of academic study. It's actually the same amount of class hours law school required me to take. Then, in 2017, I re-launched my firm to focus specifically on the estate planning and business planning needs of small business owners and entrepreneurs.

My Hope Is That This Book Will Give You A Great Way To Get Started

This book is important to me because I know that so many people need this information. The purpose of the book is to help those people get off the ground and get moving.

People are starting businesses left and right. Throughout the COVID-19 pandemic, people have started seriously rethinking their work habits, their desires, and their independence.

One of the things that I've seen too many times is that you usually have to choose between working with a business attorney or an estate planning attorney – the two just don't always line up. This sometimes results in needing two attorneys for your one life!

For example, we get lots of people who come to us looking for help with business planning. Then, when we ask them about estate planning, they're clueless. The same patterns often happen in reverse when we see estate planning clients who own businesses who haven't considered forming a business succession plan.

What most people don't realize is how much of their wealth is tied up in their business and what that could mean for them and their families if something happens to them.

The number of business owners who don't have this type of planning done is significantly higher than the number of business owners who have started a plan of any kind – yet more and more businesses are opening and closing their doors every day. On average, about 600,000 just close every year. Only 20% of businesses that are listed for sale actually sell.

If people had a better idea of where to start, what to do, and what questions to ask, we'd see many more opportunities for success across the board. My goal for the book is to give business owners like you a starting point so that you can choose how to move forward with strategic and tactical information.

If you ask me, small businesses are the economic backbone of this country. The American dream is born and realized through small businesses. In the most recent generation, small businesses created 2/3 of the jobs in the United States.

So as we say around my firm, "How can we help?" My hope is that this book is one way for us to help – so that you can get started, no matter where you are along the way.

CHAPTER 1

THE IMPORTANCE OF ESTATE AND BUSINESS PLANNING

The Deep Connection Between Business Planning and Estate Planning

Business and estate planning intertwine at the core level of wealth.

While estate planning focuses on questions like: "These are all my assets – how do I make sure that I can pass them on while retaining the highest value of my efforts?" Business planning focuses on questions like: "How is my business organized?" and "What will happen to my business in the future?"

Most businesses in the United States simply close when a person passes away. They just wrap up and are done – and the customers get left hanging.

Accordingly, if you have built your wealth and assets through a business and don't have a plan in place, the wealth and the assets that you may think will be passed on through your estate plan simply won't be there.

Without A Plan, You Risk Everything

For example, a client of mine is a very successful surgeon.

While the surgeon's spouse contributes to the business end of the practice, he doesn't contribute to the bottom line of the business in the sense that he is not the one performing surgeries.

So if the surgeon can't work in the practice anymore, all that revenue goes away. How will the family meet expenses? Plus, the accumulated wealth can disappear and the intangible value of the practice can evaporate.

In this situation, what would the surgeon, his spouse, and their family be left with? Unfortunately, very little, if anything.

Most business owners look at their business as a retirement plan – holding an idea such as: "I'll build this enterprise up and then I'll sell it. Then, the money earned from the sale will be the financial legacy I leave to my family."

The thing is, there are countless questions that come alongside this plan that few business owners actually consider. Like, "When do you want to sell your business?" "How will you make sure that you get the greatest value from this asset?" And more. . .

The problem is this: Without estate and business plans in place, your business will be vulnerable to whatever default settings are in your state's law.

A Look Into The Statistics

A Forbes article published in 2019 states that "two-thirds of all Americans" don't have a Healthcare Directive.

In 2022, Caring.com conducted a survey on wills that included nearly 3,000 adults aged 18 and older. This survey showed that:

- 66.9% of Americans don't have a Will.
- 1 out of 3 Americans doesn't have an estate plan because they feel they have too little to leave behind.
- 63% of Americans who make more than $80,000 or more a year cited "procrastination" as their reason for not having a Will.

In The Exit Planning Institute's 2013 Readiness Survey, small business owners reported that:

- 2/3 are not familiar with their exit options.
- 78% have no formal transition team.
- 83% have no written transition plan.
- 49% have done no planning at all.

- 40% have no plans in place to cover illness, death, or forced exit.
- 1/2 feel ownership transition plans require the company to remain profitable for the plans to be properly executed, but. . .
    - 86% have not taken on a strategic review or a value enhancement project.
    - 56% felt they had a good idea of what their business is worth, but. . .
    - Only 18% have had a formal valuation in the last two years.

Note that updates of this data from regional Exit Planning Institute chapters show that not much has changed in about a decade.

The Danger Of Waiting

One client of mine is a small auto body shop owner and mechanic. We got into contact when he came to my office looking to start a business succession plan.

This individual was in their mid-70s, had a few lucrative contracts with local car dealerships, and was looking to transition out of his business - because the proceeds of the sale would be his retirement plan.

Unfortunately, the business owner died during the consultation phase. So there was no way that his business was going to be worth much of anything compared to when the mechanic was alive.

The main difference was that the company's "going concern" value was worth a little shy of half-a-million dollars — even as a very simple body shop.

But once the business owner passed away, the business wasn't worth that "going concern" value anymore. Instead, it was only worth the "book value" of the shop's assets such as the machinery and real estate.

These two concepts, "going concern" and "book value", are very different from the valuation standpoint. A "going concern" value is based on the business continuing indefinitely and being profitable. But why the difference from "book value"?

Well, you can think about it in a simple way. . .

When it comes to the "book value"[1], the worth of the assets is similarly determined by asking a question like: "What would you pay for used auto repair equipment at a garage sale?"

Not only that, the "garage sale" process for the sale of assets after death is something you may have heard of before . . .

It's called Probate.

Is Your Business Prepared For Probate?

For business owners without a plan, Probate can be a double whammy – and in some cases, it can even be a triple whammy.

This is because the first part of the Probate is a court process in which the court takes the supervisory position over the decedent's assets. (The "decedent" is the person who owned the assets but has now passed away.)

---

[1] Book value is how much the company's assets are worth on the balance sheet, less the company's liabilities.

This supervisory position is taken with the purpose of paying the creditors first – and the estate and heirs second.

The "first whammy" of Probate is time. Probate cases can take anywhere from 9 - 14 months even for the most simple, uncontested matters.

The "second whammy" of Probate is cost. Probate will cost you attorney's fees – and it also costs you when it comes to valuation.

Valuation is the process in which you determine how much the assets in an estate are worth. You have to pay for someone to perform these valuations – which is especially unfortunate when this process can be avoided altogether.

(And, yes—a business is considered an asset.)

The "third whammy" of probate is the way that it can quickly drain the value of your estate.

Between the attorney's fees and valuation fees, a massive hit can be taken by the loss of the business owner. When a business owner passes away without a plan, it causes the value of the business to plummet.[2]

This means that after both time and money have gone out the door to pay the professionals and complete the probate process, the family is left to take the hit.

That's why this planning is so critical. Without it, your family — the people that you always had at the forefront of your mind to provide a better life for — are left with so much less, if they are left with anything at all.

So what can you do?

It's Important To Learn Everything You Can

Business and estate planning starts with figuring out your goals and then "digging in" to find out exactly what that means for you.

---

[2] For professionals like engineers, doctors, and attorneys, there's a fourth whammy out there too. If the professional passes away, the professional practice business might have to close because there is not anyone else qualified to operate it.

One of my mentors teaches this: "Yes is nothing without how."

What does that mean? Let's use an example. Consider that you are looking to buy a house. You say, "Yes, I will buy that house." But what you should really be able to say is, "This is how I will buy that house, with cash and financing."

When a business owner says, "Yes, I want to maximize the value of my business." The following question, (and the one that they typically haven't thought about) is: "How are you going to do that?"

The way we find the answers to these "how" questions is by being thoughtful and attentive. It's hard to know where to start on your own. Working with an expert attorney will always give you the best answers, and therefore, the best results.

How Planning Can Help You Enjoy Your Wealth While You're Still Alive

Too many people avoid planning because they consider it to be a dark subject. Conversations that surround what will happen to everything you've worked for once you've passed away aren't necessarily the most pleasant ones to have. It doesn't have to be this way.

Something that few people even consider is the ways in which planning can help you enjoy your wealth during your lifetime by finding peace of mind and being able to watch your children benefit.

When I talk to my clients about planning in this way, I always see their eyes light up.

People are more than their assets. I haven't met a single person who has ever said, "I was just overjoyed by getting my aunt's diamond ring after she died."

People are focused on the memories they have with people. What I hear most often are things like, "When I was growing up, Aunt Mary would come to visit every two weeks. It was amazing. When she was there, we did so many things and had so many great experiences."

The majority of people want the experience more than they want the money. When a successful business owner is able to leverage all their good work and use it during their lifetime to teach their kids the value of what it takes to get this done – it is unbelievably beneficial.

CHAPTER 2

HOW I AM PREPARED TO HELP

My Military Experience Helped Me Become A Natural Planner

One of the key values I learned as a Marine officer is that your job is to think about every contingency and make a plan for all of them. The concept is called mission-oriented planning.

(If you're interested, a version of this thought process is explained by Stephen Covey in his book, The Seven Habits of Highly Effective People.)

One lesson that my experience as a former Marine and commercial litigator taught me is that you have to keep in mind both the soft and hard aspects of contingency planning. In other words, you have to make sure that you have a strategy for anything that comes your way.

If you think to yourself, "Well, I'm successful, so I'm protected." You leave yourself vulnerable to unforeseen events that can strike anyone.

For the most part, this way of thinking doesn't work. Because the "yes" plan that you have in place is only as strong as the "how" plan that you have set up for whatever catastrophe could ever pass your way. Hope is not a plan.

This is one of the core reasons I went into estate planning law after years as a commercial litigator. My experience as a strategic and operations planner in the Marine Corps showed me what one of my mentors put into words so clearly years later: "Yes is nothing without how."

In my time in the military, I would encounter situations where a commander would present a plan of attack. It was my job to ask and plan for all the questions that needed to follow. . .

"How am I supposed to get you water?"

"What about food?"

"What about extra ammunition?"

"How long are you going to be there?"

If you take these concepts into estate planning – it's easy to see how important the "how" is to the "yes".

A business owner will often say something like, "I want to sell my business in three years for seven times earnings before interest, taxes, depreciation, and amortization." [3]

---

[3] "EBITDA" is a popular method of determining the value of a business.

This is a great aspirational goal. How do you get there? How do you find a strategy that provides you with the security to withstand any unexpected events that may come up along the way?

The Benefit Of Working With Someone Who Is Trained To Handle A Crisis

Many people know that by working with a business lawyer, who is also a veteran, you are working with someone who has both a high level of attention to detail and dedication to service. But what few understand about working with a military veteran is that we are all taught how to manage conflict, chaos, and uncertainty with a level head.

There have been countless times when a client has contacted me in a state of distress – explaining that their situation is completely out of control. While many people might get thrown off by this kind of phone call, I and other veterans/attorneys are able to take these things in stride.

One example of this is a time when my unit was doing pre-deployment training in 1997 off the coast of Southern California.

While we were at sea, a bunch of sailors and Marines was standing on a catwalk underneath the flight deck, which was about 150 feet in the air in the middle of the Pacific Ocean when, all of the sudden, a guy on a jet ski pulls up to the ship and asked, "Hey! Can someone tell me which way to California?"

We soon learned that this man and his three friends had rented jet skis and were lost at sea. Immediately, our training exercise shifted to a real-life operation where the ship's search and rescue team had to jump into action.

Fortunately, we found two of the three lost men pretty quickly . . . but it took nearly eight hours to find the fourth jet skier. When the helicopter pilots finally spotted the last jet skier, he was slumped over the jet ski – passed out and suffering from exposure.

As you can see, adapting to an unplanned emergency situation is a key aspect of our training.

When the first jet skier came up to the ship, we had a hundred other things happening during our actual training exercise. Then, we had to put that training immediately into practice to save a man's life.

At my firm, one of our core values is that we are always learning and training.

In our practice, there are always new rules coming out for tax law, business law, and estate law, at both the state and federal levels, that can require adjustments to someone's plan. This means that when a client calls us, terrified that these new circumstances will throw their plans into a tailspin, we have the structure in place to make those changes.

In the Marine Corps, we were taught never to be static in our training, our education, our athleticism, and more. This transfers directly to my work as an attorney. We are always sharpening the saw.[4] We understand that businesses evolve, so attorneys should evolve too. Because we're always planning for contingencies, we're ready for anything that comes our way.

OODA: Observe, Orient, Decide, Act

Among countless other systems, the military uses one key tool for remaining flexible in crisis. This is called the OODA loop.

OODA stands for Observe, Orient, Decide, Act. The system was developed by a fighter pilot with the intention of winning high-intensity in-air battles. In theory, whichever pilot could perform the OODA loop cycle with the greatest speed and accuracy would be the pilot that survived.

This applies to businesses when it comes to:

- Bringing a product to market;
- Competing with other companies;

---

[4] Covey, Stephen R. The 7 Habits of Highly Effective People, 298 (15th Anniversary Ed. Kindle 2013).

- Managing employees;
- Making time for your family;
- Planning for taxes down the road;
- And more . . .

The faster a business owner can get through the OODA loop, the more successful their business will be. With my veteran experience, it comes naturally to help my business clients get through the OODA loop faster.

One of the most important parts of my role as your attorney is my ability to give you a bird's eye view of your operation. As someone who is independent, I can come in with fresh eyes and see things differently than someone who is working every day in this team effort.

In military parlance, you might think of yourself, the business owner, as the commander, while thinking about your business attorney as an advisor and planner. You get to decide what you want to do operationally, and my role is to make sure that it can be executed seamlessly by orchestrating the plan to account for any number of unexpected scenarios.

Conquering Fear

There are countless moments in Marine Corps training during which you have to overcome your inherent fear.

12 years into my service in the Marine Corps, I joined an airborne unit. Part of our training required us to learn how to jump out of planes and into areas of active combat. During this time, my commander was particularly keen on parachuting. So, he required all of our team members – the officers and non-commissioned officers alike – to go to Airborne ("Jump") School.

Honestly, I am not a fan of heights – but I had to overcome my fear of stepping out of a perfectly good aircraft to continue on my path in the military.

Similarly, the entrepreneur's journey is not a straight one, the path to success constantly goes forward, backward, diagonally, and backward again. The thing is, fear is an inherent part of every business owner's day-to-day life. It's being able to recognize and understand the existence of this fear that allows you to overcome it.

CHAPTER 3

PREPARING FOR THE "WHAT-IFS"

People come to our firm at different stages on their business journey from start-up clients who are looking to build their empire on a strong foundation, to people who have built a successful business on a house of cards, and yet others who have put the time in and are ready to step away.

No matter who you are or where you are going, it's crucial that you have a plan in place to protect yourself and your efforts from all of life's "what-ifs".

How A Plan Can Relieve Your Worry About Life's "What-Ifs"

So many people don't have a plan in place for the "what-ifs". . .

What if you get in an accident when you leave your house today?

What if you find yourself stuck in another country because of a global pandemic?

What if you can't pick your kids up from school?

What if your business partner files for divorce?

Few people like to think about how things might go wrong — but you have to wonder, wouldn't you feel less stressed about these "what-ifs" if you had a plan in place to deal with the situation before it ever happened?

Estate and business planning gives you the opportunity to know that you have a strategy in place for any kind of crisis. There is no "right time" to get this work done, but each day you wait is another day that you leave yourself vulnerable to a host of catastrophes.

What's more, you need to continue to readjust your plan in line with the OODA loop principles in mind so that you can stay prepared as your life continues to change.

You may think to yourself, "I have a plan, so I'm protected! I met with an attorney years ago and have a binder with documents to prove it."

What if that was 10 years ago?

What if, since then, you've added another three children and $500,000 in profit to your life?

Without altering your old plan, the entire 10 years of life that you've lived since then likely won't be accounted for or included. This means your assets could be subject to probate, your beneficiaries could be left without an inheritance, and your past wishes for healthcare could be honored, even though you've changed your mind since then.

Understanding What Happens When The "What Ifs" Hit You Unprepared

Probate is what will happen to your *"stuff"* if you don't have an estate plan in place when you pass away. Through the probate process, you effectively sue yourself — or, your personal representative sues you - to repay your creditors post-mortem.

What does this mean? During probate, the courts will take on the administration of your estate to pay your creditors first.

This is especially vital to understand if you are a business owner who doesn't have an estate plan in place, as the value of your business will usually plummet once you're gone. That means that the money you thought you had to leave to your family might not be there.

For example, if you planned to leave $4 million to your family and pass away without a plan — it may be the case that all the money you had "set aside" to keep your family taken care of could drop to as low as $400,000.

This isn't even the greatest risk that your loved ones could face . . .

Consider this "what-if": You go out to dinner with your spouse and both of you get into a fatal car accident – What would happen to your children? The 16-year-old babysitter that you left them with certainly wouldn't be able to step in as a parent on your behalf. So, now what?

In this situation, the custody of your minor children would be taken over by the state and your kids would be placed into foster care until a suitable long-term guardian is found for them.

If you have a business partner the questions could be:

What will happen to the value of your business if there's ever a divorce?

If your partner gets divorced, do you want to be in business with their ex-spouse?

What if the two of you get into a disagreement that you can't find a compromise on?

What if either of you were ever to become disabled?

Fortunately, most small business owners are candidates for trust-based planning. Even if a plan was made in the past, I frequently see business owners with some type of trust-based plan in place that needs further attention and planning. *Why is this?*

Most small businesses in the U.S. are organized as an S-corporation for tax purposes. This is where the revenue and expenses of the business pass onto the business owner(s) personally. In these cases, the business is not taxed separately – it's taxed through the owner's personal tax return.

If you plan on putting your small business into a trust, you need to keep this in mind: **S-corporations cannot be owned by a trust except for in very specific circumstances.** When those specific circumstances are not met, the structure that was in place will fall apart, the S-election will be lost, and the taxes can go up astronomically and immediately.

How To Build A Plan That Will Start Benefiting You NOW

Our approach to estate planning is that it should always benefit you during your lifetime – and not only when you pass away.

There is so much to look forward to between the time that you begin planning and the end of your life. Why make a plan that won't benefit you while you are alive to enjoy it?

Many people will create a Will with the intention of protecting their estate from probate. But not only is a Will rarely enough of a plan for a business owner's needs, it only takes effect once you've passed away.

On the other hand, Revocable Living Trust planning can benefit you and your family both during your life and after. How? Because plans with a Revocable Living Trust include protections for any potential crisis.

This is so important to me because I know personally how critical it is to have a plan for the unexpected. What if my wife's cancer treatment was unsuccessful? I'm humbled at the position it would have left our family in.

What's more, I want to help others find ways to protect all of their assets. This way, you can pass on your financial wealth and the wealth of knowledge and experience that you've gained along your entrepreneurship journey.

CHAPTER 4

WHAT MAKES UP A COMPLETE ESTATE PLAN?

Each estate plan is as unique as the person who creates it. That said, there are standard documents that will be adjusted to create and customize the plan that best suits your individual needs.

Your Estate Plan should include a:

- Revocable Living Trust
- Pour-Over Will
- Special Power of Attorney

- Durable Power of Attorney
- Healthcare Power of Attorney
- Advance Healthcare Directive (Living Will)
- HIPAA Authorization
- Declaration of Pre-Need Guardian
- And possibly more . . .

Below, you can find a description of each of these Estate Planning tools, along with an explanation of their purpose, function, and importance.

Revocable Living Trusts

A Revocable Living Trust is an estate planning tool with many benefits.

Primarily, these trusts are used to:

- Avoid Probate
- Protect Your Assets
- Reduce Excess Taxation
- Ensure That Your Heirs Can Access Their Inheritance

- Guide Your Heirs even after you've passed away.

These trusts are "revocable" because they can be changed during your lifetime. These trusts are relatively simple to set up and can protect your legacy both during your lifetime and after you've passed away.

The Revocable Living Trust ("RLT") is the essential foundational document for a business owner. It allows for smoother management of assets, including the business, both during the business owner's lifetime and after their death. A more detailed examination of the benefits and importance of RLT-based planning is in Chapter 6.

There's another type of broad category of trusts called irrevocable trusts. These are used in all sorts of situations: for large life insurance policies, to own pieces of a business or investment company, to make charitable and non-charitable gifts, and to restructure tax liability. Irrevocable trust planning may be appropriate for some people, but only after they finish their foundational planning.

Wills & Pour-Over Wills

At the bare minimum, everyone should have a Will.

The purpose of a Will is to give the court instructions regarding how you wish your estate to be distributed after your creditors are paid.

The Will is an essential part of every Estate Plan because it creates "rules" for your assets that take into consideration all of the unique aspects of your situation. Why is this important? Because each state has its own set of rules for the distribution of an estate. This means that if you die without a Will, (this is called "dying intestate"), your assets will be distributed based on the laws of the land. As we like to say, "if you don't have a plan, the state has one for you".

To illustrate how the state's plan might not be the best one for you, consider what happens if you have a blended family. (If you're not familiar with this term, a blended family refers to families with stepchildren and stepparents from other marriages.)

If you have a blended family and you die intestate, the state will not pass your assets to someone that is not related to you by blood. Alternatively, your Will superseded the state law default setting and ensures that everyone you care about is taken care of by your estate after you pass away.

It's important to keep in mind: There is a lot of focus on Will-based planning, but if you only have a Will in your Estate Plan, you won't be able to take advantage of the many lifetime benefits of estate planning.

This is because a Will only takes effect after you have passed away. What's more, Wills are rarely enough on their own to ensure that business owners have the complete protections that a comprehensive Estate Plan can provide.

Pour-Over Wills

The Pour-Over Will is slightly different from a standalone Will in that it is created in conjunction with an RLT. It acts as a "safety net" for the RLT. Pour-Over

Wills have multiple advantages, including their simplicity, comprehensiveness, and relative privacy.

By combining all of the instructions within a trust into one document, it's easy for estate administration to go smoothly.

What's more, if you're not able to transfer a recently acquired asset into your RLT, the Pour-Over Will catches into your trust estate. Also, the contents of the Pour-Over Will are usually quite vague because the more detailed instructions are in the RLT.

There is a great number of circumstances that can change the way that your estate plan is formed and revised over the years. The most important thing is that you take the time to put these provisions into place, and then update them to reflect your goals and needs as life changes throughout the years.

Powers Of Attorney

A Power of Attorney allows you to appoint someone you trust as an "agent" for a particular task or to manage a particular asset. What does this mean?

For example, consider that you are traveling abroad and you lose your bank card. In this situation, you could contact your Power of Attorney. Because of their legal authority to take action on your behalf, they could send you money from your own bank account. Another popular use of a Power of Attorney is to get the title for your car when you purchase it from a dealership.

These types of Powers of Attorney are called limited or special powers of attorney. This is a great lifetime planning tool – it can ensure that you have access to particular assets in an unexpected situation that you cannot personally access yourself.

Durable Power Of Attorney

The Durable Power of Attorney is an absolutely essential document for anyone. This document is similar to the Power of Attorney described above, but it has one important distinction . . .

Just as with a Power of Attorney, you will appoint someone you trust to manage your assets and finances on your behalf.

The difference is that a Durable Power of Attorney remains in effect even if you are incapacitated. Many limited or special powers of attorney become ineffective upon the incapacity of the principal (you).

If you are medically incapacitated, the person who is appointed as your Durable Power of Attorney can make sure that your financial and related matters are attended to, your property is maintained, and more.

Healthcare Power Of Attorney

In your Healthcare Power of Attorney, you will appoint a trusted friend or family member to make medical decisions on your behalf.

This can include decisions regarding the use of certain medications, operations, or life-sustaining machines.

Advance Healthcare Directive (Also Called: Living Will)

Your Advance Healthcare Directive (or, Living Will) is a document that allows you to dictate your wishes for medical treatment and life-sustaining procedures. This is referred to in the event that you become permanently incapacitated (i.e, If your body is alive, but your brain is not functioning).

This document is similar to a Healthcare Power of Attorney, but instead of giving someone the authority to make medical decisions on your behalf – it directly outlines how you would like your care to be handled in the event of a terminal or similar health situation.

Everyone should have a Living Will. It is a critical document that gives caregivers, medical providers, and loved ones instructions on "what to do" if you enter a persistent vegetative state. A "persistent vegetative state" is also referred to as post-coma unresponsiveness (PCU). You've probably heard of this referred to as the state of being "brain dead".

The importance of a Living Will is clear – especially when you consider some of the events that have come about when a person doesn't have a Living Will in place . . .

The Terri Schiavo Case

The most renowned story of this kind occurred in 1990 when Terri Schaivo suffered a massive cardiac arrest in her Florida home.

After Schiavo was resuscitated, it was found that she had suffered significant brain damage from a lack of oxygen to her brain. These injuries caused Schiavo to remain comatose for two and a half months. Her diagnosis then was changed to reflect the persistent vegetative state. She remained in this state for the rest of her life.

What does this have to do with a Living Will? Schiavo did not have an Advance Healthcare Directive. So when her husband, Michael, disagreed with her parents' decision to keep her on life support after two years of unsuccessful treatment - he had to go to court.

It wasn't until 2005, a full 14 years later, that the case was finally resolved. This tragedy kept Terri's family in an unending hurricane of misery for over a decade.

Schiavo was only 26 years old when she suffered the heart attack that set this story into motion. It's no wonder that, at such a young age, Terri didn't have a Living Will in place – she had probably never started to consider Estate Planning.

But her story shows us why it's never too soon to start thinking about protecting yourself and your loved ones with a plan.

HIPAA Authorizations

Under the Health Insurance Portability and Accountability Act of 1996 (more commonly referred to as HIPAA), healthcare providers are prohibited from discussing your medical care with anyone you have not authorized them to speak with.

You'll want to provide HIPAA authorization for anyone that you would want your doctors to be able to discuss your care with.

As a side note: *Your Durable Power of Attorney, Healthcare Power of Attorney, and Living Will should all work hand-in-hand.*

Declaration Of Pre-Need Guardian

All parents with minor children should have a Declaration of Pre-Need Guardian. This is a document that protects your children from entering the foster care system in the event that both parents are unable to care for their children because of death, illness, and more.

The name of this document will vary from state to state, but its function will remain the same.

In your Declaration of Pre-Need Guardian, you will appoint the emergency care of your child(ren) to a specific person such as a grandparent, aunt or uncle, or godparent on either a permanent or temporary basis.

CHAPTER 5

WHEN YOU SHOULD REVIEW YOUR PLAN. . . AND WHY

There are countless situations that might change your estate planning needs. So it's essential to review your estate plan once every few years to account for any of the life changes that you will experience along the way.

For example, consider this story . . .

I helped a client of mine form an estate plan with his wife. At the time, he had recently started a business and the young couple was only just starting to talk about having children.

His initial estate plan was not very complex and, of course, it didn't account for any heirs or large assets.

Three years later, he came to my office to review his plan. But by this time, he and his wife had children and their business had grown to generate a few million in yearly revenue.

Because of his change in circumstances, we needed to perform a complete overhaul of the documents and protections in place. If you consider this client's situation, it is easy to understand the importance of reviewing your plan . . .

Our basic rule is that you should review your estate plan every three years – unless a major life change prompts you to do so sooner. Estate plans are very easy to change with the help of your attorney. This way, you can account for changes like:

- New Family Members
- New Assets

- Business Growth
- And More. . .

How To Ensure That Your Plan Is Going To Work

Conceptually speaking, many business owners have a contingency plan in place. But, in actuality, few people have the structure needed to ensure their plans are legally secure.

When estate planning with your business in mind, you'll want to consider the "Five D's of What-If Planning":

- Death
- Disability
- Divorce
- Disagreement
- Distress

You never want to assume that the assets you have put into your business will be inherently protected. Instead, you should work with an attorney who can ensure that you have a robust legal structure of security so that you are protected from the "Five D's" – and any other emergency that may come your way.

Are You Positive That Your Plan Is Ready For Anything?

Once, I met some clients in a restaurant to go over their estate and business plan. I asked what documents they had in place. The wife was obviously happy to provide a binder full of entity documents and other legal paperwork – she handed it over, proud that she was already a step ahead.

As I started going over the documents, you could see her demeanor shift as it became apparent that the paperwork I had in front of me was nothing close to the bulletproof security she thought it would be.

The documents seemed to come from Mad-Libs®. I could see that the couple likely obtained form documents and filled them out to the best of their ability -- but there were gaping holes all over the paperwork. Sections detailing the business name, the names of shareholders, the principal place of business, and the purpose of the business were left completely blank.

You could see that the couple truly believed they already had a leg-up on this process, but their legal security was in jeopardy. This was through no fault of their own but was only due to the fact that they didn't have the legal expertise needed to create the structure that is the cornerstone of these efforts. You don't know what you don't know.

The thing is, if this couple had never hired an attorney, they may never have known the problems that arise from a poorly-constructed plan at first hand.

Consider The Cautionary Tale Of A Father Who Left Things The Way They Were

Not too long ago, I was the corporate attorney for clients who were involved in probate and trust litigation matters.

In this case, the father of three children had started an LLC (Limited Liability Company) in Florida. This LLC owned a commercial property in Chicago, the legal planning was done by an attorney in Illinois, and the plan hadn't been updated since its creation.

One day, the man's daughter passed away, leaving behind her husband and two brothers. Years after that, the elder brother went on to become the father's primary caregiver.

During this time, the father transferred ownership of the Florida LLC over to the eldest brother. While there was an estate plan in place, it was left unaltered. Therefore, the younger brother and the deceased sister's family and children were left out.

So when the father passed away, the largest asset in his estate went to a sole heir — the eldest brother.

This created a massive legal dispute within the family. The commercial property in Chicago was worth nearly $10 million. The attorney who created the estate plan 25 years ago had long since retired and couldn't be contacted. The estate plan didn't account for the business transfer and the LLC operating agreement (which included the transfer) was full of holes. The family suffered greatly from this. There were fights, and deep wounds, and each party had to spend an incredible amount of time and money to resolve the matter.

Prior to his passing, the father was in relatively good health. He certainly had the time and the resources to alter his plan – but he didn't take advantage of this opportunity.

But imagine how radically different this story would be if he had made changes throughout his life. Imagine that, after his daughter's passing, he contacted an estate planning attorney to ensure that his grandchildren would be included as heirs.

Imagine what might have happened if, when he transferred the LLC to his eldest son, he had his attorney adjust the operating agreement to secure his other children's claim to the Chicago property.

If he had made other decisions, you'd likely never hear this story – because it wouldn't be a cautionary tale. Instead, it likely would have been an easy process for his family who wouldn't have needed to reach out to me and file a lawsuit in the first place.

CHAPTER 6

HOW TO PROTECT YOUR BUSINESS WITH ESTATE PLANNING

A business owner should be attentive to several different aspects of legal planning that will best ensure their business continues for as long as they wish.

Succession Planning

Succession Planning is the process through which a business owner creates a legal framework to transfer the operations and ownership of the business to their family or a third party. This planning will also account for the situation if the owner/operator becomes incapacitated.

Many families can benefit from Succession Planning. However, you have to keep in mind that not every family member will want to go into the business. Neither is every family member's right for the business.

History can show us two versions of the succession story in which one famous family learned from the travails of the other's succession story. Salvatore Ferragamo founded Ferragamo by making women's footwear. Although Salvatore passed away in 1960, his wife Wanda stayed active in the business and continued the company's growth. As icons of the Italian fashion industry, the Ferragamo Family watched as the Gucci family suffered incredible strife and loss as a result of their succession plans.

The Gucci family's chaos unfolded "across the street". Wanda decided that this would never happen in their family. As a result, they created a succession plan with two main protections in mind:

- *No more than three members of the family are legally allowed to work in the company at any given time;*
- *No spouses could work within the main business.*

Salvatore and Wanda Ferragamo had several children, (many of whom were married), and many grandchildren. You've probably never heard of the inner workings of their business – but that's the point. Their succession plan created a structure that prevented the high drama that is common fodder for gossip, movies, and more.

You might think that "These succession rules are very specific" yes, they are. This is the concept at the very core of succession planning. You can create a highly-tailored plan that is custom fit to your family, your concerns, and your goals for the future. How? By working with an attorney who has the expertise needed to create a plan that will stand the test of time.

Creditor Protection Planning

Depending on how your business is organized, you should consider planning that will protect your personal assets from business debts. Simultaneously, you might consider tools that will protect your business assets from your personal debt.

Absent these protections, your personal assets and business(es) may be vulnerable to probate claims and liability claims. These assets would repay your creditors, instead of supporting the people you love.

Tax Planning

Anyone looking to get the greatest value out of their business will need to create a tax strategy that can protect their business from excessive taxation.

This is best done when the business owner is still alive and able to actively contribute to their business. The value of a business can drop significantly when the business owner passes away. Therefore, lifetime tax planning provides the best opportunity to minimize exposure to taxation and maximize the value of your assets.

Among other things you can plan for:

- Income Tax
- Capital Gains Tax
- Estate Tax
- Transfer Tax
- Generation Skip Planning

Incapacity Planning

Owning your own business can open up an entirely new way of living. I found this out firsthand when I changed my life to pursue business ownership and gained control over my time again. But what happens to my business if I suffered a traumatic injury that made me unable to practice law? *What would happen to my family?*

One of the greatest dangers that any business owner faces is those situations that would cause the business to stop functioning.

This can happen in many different ways, but the repercussions are all too common. If a business owner becomes incapacitated, everything can grind to a halt. The family income could disappear and the whole business might fall apart.

Of course, you may be able to find someone to take over your daily operations, but how would you do this if you are already dealing with some kind of severe medical trauma?

If I think about how this would apply to my situation as an attorney, I have to ask myself these questions:

Whom could I trust to run my business for me?

Would my clients want to work with someone else?

How could I ask them to trust someone they've never met?

At the very least, this person would be hand-selected by me to fulfill my role, but these matters require a herculean amount of faith in both you as a business owner and your clients or buyers who have grown to trust you and your services over time.

What if you are an architect? Or what if you provide some artistic service that can't be replicated by someone else?

As soon as you start asking these questions, you can see how essential incapacity planning becomes.

Of course, no one plans to experience a life-altering injury – or, at the very least, to be put "out of commission", even for a period of time, but you can't ensure that these situations will never happen.

What you can do is have a protective strategy in place in case the worst-case scenario happens.

A Case Study You'll Never Forget

In the early 2000s, there was a boutique law firm in Miami that worked internationally. At its peak, the firm boasted nearly 70 attorneys and rented an office on the top floor of one of the most prominent buildings in the heart of downtown Miami.

The firm was started by one attorney and it still only used his name. Their success seemed unstoppable, but there was a problem.

This firm possessed legal experts who specialized in nearly every area of the law. But, there was no succession plan in place. When the firm's founder and sole shareholder passed away, the operation crumbled in a matter of minutes.

The firm was organized as a PA (a "professional association") with a single owner. Once the sole owner died, there was no structure for the business to continue operating. It was gone immediately. Not a single one of the 70 other attorneys could lawfully represent or support the firm's clients.

If you had a bird's eye view of the situation, it would be easy for you to liken it to the chaos of a 6-year-old's birthday party gone wrong. . . "Everyone was running around in a mania, but nothing was actually getting done."

You may think, "Okay, but this was a major law firm. What about my small business? What about my commercial enterprise?"

Consider this: If your business is structured as a sole proprietorship, what happens if the sole proprietor is unable to fulfill their role?

Any company would come to a screeching halt if the sole proprietor were to become incapacitated or pass away. For professional associations, the structure is entirely based on the license holder, so when the license holder is (for whatever reason) no longer able to perform their duties . . . there's no business.

If you're wondering about the Yolofsky Law succession plan, we have addressed this to ensure there is continuity with our clients.

Make Sure That You Have An Attorney You Can Rely On

Here's a dark secret about how some estate planning attorneys work.

The dirty little secret about the estate planning industry is that attorneys will create a Will for the business owner and say "All right, you're covered".

But, remember, a Will only works in one situation – when you die. So when that Will passes through probate, an attorney is potentially able to collect a statutory fee, based on a percentage of the value of assets that will go through probate. For example, if an attorney created a Will that covered $1 million in probate assets, they could later legitimately charge $30,000, (or 3%) as the attorney's fee for the probate.

This resulted in attorneys who would provide estate planning services at a fraction of what their hourly rate might normally be. They planned to handle probate when the time came. They would create plans that structured assets such that the probate "price tag" would be higher. When a grieving family came back for probate, just hoping to get the ball moving, they would sign onto a deal that added a significant price tag to the attorney's benefit.

Fortunately, Florida recently changed these laws. Now, an attorney must first disclose to the heirs that they intend to charge the statutory rate and they have to find the approval of these terms. If they don't, the attorney can't proceed under the statutory rate.

This is one of the reasons that trust-based planning is so vital. These services are a bit more expensive up front, but they are an investment. Not only can trust-based planning give you the peace of mind that comes with knowing your loved ones will be cared for — it can all but eliminate the probate process.

What You Should Know About Trust-Based Planning

- A trust-based plan eliminates a significant amount (if not all) of the probate process.
- If a business owner's estate plan is done correctly on the front end, the back end cost should be much lower.
- There are attorney fees to administer a trust after a person passes away, however, those fees can be negotiated.
- There can be a statutory percentage fee associated with trust administration.
- There is no way to probate a Will except through court, however. Trust administration does not usually require court supervision. Indeed, it might never see a court.
- A Will does not create a safety net for incapacity. Meanwhile, trust-based planning can provide lifetime benefits and crisis relief.
- A trust-based plan can create provisions for your successor in conjunction with securing the structure of your business entity.

The Benefits Of Trust-Based Succession Planning For Your Business

Consider the following situation. You are in business with a partner who is not a relative of yours. One day, your business partner passes away unexpectedly. Fortunately, you both set up a business succession plan.

Under the plan, you have agreed that in this situation you will buy your partner's interest in the company from their family. This "buy price" has been predetermined and agreed upon by you and your partner in advance, so there is no need to perform a valuation of the company. According to the plan, you purchase the deceased partner's interest from the family.

Here, the operations of the business carry on uninterrupted. What's more, your partner's family is fairly compensated.

Of course, these kinds of plans are completely unique to each enterprise and each business relationship. But this is just another reason why you cannot overemphasize the benefit of a seasoned and experienced planning attorney.

Pro tip: these types of arrangements are called Buy/Sell agreements. The cash to pay for the deceased's interest is usually obtained from life insurance.

CHAPTER 7

WHAT ASSET PROTECTION PLANNING REALLY MEANS

Asset protection are two words that are ubiquitous in the industry among planners, attorneys, and clients. The idea behind asset protection is this:

"I have an asset, a business, a boat, a second house, or an investment account that I want to protect from creditors' claims."

Most commonly, asset protection is associated with real estate – and especially the commercial or rental property that provides the venue for a person's business. However, the idea is to separate the income-generating asset from other assets. This is especially important for professional practices.

For example, I might have a client who runs a consulting business in Fort Lauderdale but owns a beach condo in Clearwater (on the west coast of Florida state). This client wants to protect their condo from claims against their business. And likewise, they want to protect their business from any claims against the condo. This is where "asset protection" comes into play.

Know that every claimant will investigate publicly available information to determine what assets might be used to satisfy a judgment against you. Typically, this is done by a creditor's rights attorney or a personal injury lawyer.

For example, if someone were looking to obtain compensation for a medical malpractice lawsuit against a surgeon, their attorney would perform an investigation to see what assets that surgeon has available to satisfy the claim. This is especially true if the "surgeon" has no insurance – such as malpractice coverage.

The question that this investigation is trying to answer is simple: "Do you have access to the assets, finances, or resources to cover the dollar value of this claim?

Creditors' Claims Can Sink The Ship

What separates creditors' claims from any other claim is that a creditor's rights attorney will often use a "scorched earth" approach. This means that they will sue anyone connected with the claim, with the hopes that they find a lawsuit that "hits" and will satisfy the claim.

To do this, they may sue the individual, their attorney, accountant, financial advisor, insurance agent, and so on. The greatest benefit of this is to cast a wide net of "discovery".

Discovery is a legal term that refers to the process in any lawsuit wherein both sides are required to provide information to the other party. If a creditor's rights attorney brings legal action against anyone even remotely involved in the claim, they have a higher chance of "reeling in" evidence that would otherwise be outside of the case's jurisdiction.

For example, bringing a lawsuit against a person's attorney can supersede the "attorney-client privilege". How? Because engagement letters, contracts, and certain other legal documents may not fall within the protections you have with your attorney. Conversations between your advisors may not be privileged.

Therefore, a creditor's rights attorney may be able to find evidence of activity that plays to their favor in court – and evidence that they wouldn't have been able to obtain through any other avenue.

Another "weak spot" that is created by this wide net of creditor's rights lawsuits has to do with communications between advisors.

For example, if your insurance agent emails your attorney and accountant with information regarding asset protection planning and how insurance coverage can fit into the overall structure; it could signal that there is an asset available for the taking. Even the innocuous use of the term "asset protection" between your advisors could be blood in the water for a creditor's claim.

And once there's bait on the line for these creditors' attorneys to go after, they are relentless.

How To Make Asset Protection Planning Work For You

Based on what we've just discussed, you can likely understand why I try to avoid the term "asset protection". I don't want to leave a roadmap that suggests a relationship between one asset to another.

This doesn't mean that I won't use every tool in my box in an effort to ensure that your legacy is protected from any future contingency.

There are innovative ways to shield your efforts by hiding things in plain sight. What does this mean? It means that you can throw a creditor off the trail by structuring and documenting certain assets in such a way that they are not tied back to you.

While some people may try to make this work by creating an LLC in their spouse's or child's name – you shouldn't rely on these tactics for comprehensive protection. These are tricks that have been used time and time again and creditors will already be looking for one of these combinations.

Instead, you have to get creative. So, what can you do to really protect your assets?

You Must Understand How To Use Your LLC Properly

It's common to create an LLC that will hold your asset – instead of placing the asset directly in your name. This approach makes sense, LLCs are extremely easy to set up and there are benefits that come along with the LLC structure.

Unfortunately, many who attempt to use LLCs for asset protection aren't familiar with the concept of "Piercing the Corporate Veil". This means that, if you don't maintain all of the corporate formalities of your LLC, the court can "pierce" through the corporate entity and get to you personally. The most common way that business owners open themselves to a piercing claim is by commingling funds.

Understand What It Really Means To Pierce The Corporate Veil

John Doe owns three real estate properties, each held by a different LLC.

Property One and Property Two are successful, but Property Three is barely hanging on. If John were to take money from Business One and Business Two to cover the expenses that are being incurred by Business Three, the formality of the entire corporate structure can be destroyed.

Here, there's no corporate formality left. If you, as the owner of these assets, don't maintain the formality and separation, the court will not respect these "formality" rules later on. Therefore, the assets will be vulnerable to actions from creditors in a way that would fall outside of typical business protections.

Remember The Importance Of Maintaining Corporate Formality

In year one of planning, people are very good at maintaining the formality of their corporate structure. When year three comes around, it's easy for people to get lax and let certain things lapse.

For example, Crummey Letters are an important part of some irrevocable trusts. These Crummey Letters need to be issued every year. The failure to issue them could result in bad tax consequences. If part of the business is owned by an irrevocable trust and the letters aren't issued annually, that trust could be considered the grantor's again.

But it's not at all uncommon for a business owner and their advisor to issue these Crummey Letters in years one and two, only to let things slide once year five rolls around. Then, when it's time to sell the business held by the trust, (or when something happens to the creator of that trust), the IRS can recalculate the tax burden on the business to the year that these letters stopped being issued.

Not only does this result in a massive retroactive tax burden, but there are often penalties and interest associated with this lapse in formality.

Another quick example is the simplest and most common one, which is when the business owner uses the business as their personal piggy bank. Keeping your personal and business expenses separate helps to ensure the piercing attack doesn't win.

What You Should Know About Your Planning Defenses

While it is crucial to create legal defenses for your assets, remember that the more difficult it is for someone to break, you might find that it's similarly difficult to maintain a structure.

As such, it's crucial to have a balance between an impenetrable asset protection structure and a usable structure that insulates from liability, maintains privacy, and has tax benefits.

Additionally, these three concepts, (liability protection, privacy, and tax) are three aspects of planning that sometimes move separately. You might find that by increasing tax benefits, you might sacrifice some privacy. Sometimes, the creation of certain liability insulation structures could lead to a non-optimized tax situation.

The best course of action is to stay in regular contact with your attorney and other advisors to ensure this type of structure continues to work the way you intended.

CHAPTER 8

DO YOU HAVE AN EXIT PLAN FOR YOUR BUSINESS?

One of the most important aspects of being a business owner is having an exit strategy in place. And so often, I speak with clients who have plans for their future - but no strategy in place to put that plan into action.

If I were to ask a client, "Do you plan to work until you're 75?" They would likely respond with an emphatic, "Absolutely not!"

But if I were to then ask, "So, what is your plan for transitioning out of your business?"

Nine times out of ten I am met with a silent room and a blank stare.

This is not anyone's fault. It takes countless hours of time and attention to build an enterprise and grow a business. All this effort will usually take center stage in a person's life, making it hard to find the time to ask these questions.

Unfortunately, this means that many business owners don't have a plan for how they will transition out of work. As the classic saying goes, "the dentist dies with the drill in their hand." But this doesn't have to be you.

The truth is, there is no "right time" to start planning for the transition out of your business – but if you don't find the time, the time will find you. This may sound harsh, but it's truly not meant to be. My sole intention is to help people realize how much they have to gain by making a plan for their future.

Selling Your Business

There are many businesses that will sell – but the reality is, that most businesses just close. That's it. So, how do you know when you should look to sell your business?

The right time to sell your business is when there is an opportunity to maximize the value of your enterprise. This rarely breaks down in a way that is standard across the board.

For example, there is no rule book that says, "You should sell in month 7 between weeks 3 and 4 of year 10 of your business." Such a thing would be ridiculous. However, evaluating your business's performance can give you the information you need to make this important decision.

One of the many aspects of this evaluation is understanding EBITDA.

EBITDA stands for Earnings Before Interest, Taxes, Depreciation, and Amortization. It is the measure of a company's comprehensive financial performance.

Another measure of this evaluation is your "multiple". Essentially, it allows you to "multiply" your revenue by a number that is determined by comparing your assets to those of other companies on the market that are similar to yours.

So, for example, consider that you want to sell your business and net $5 million; you are generating $2 million in revenue; your EBITDA measures $600,000; and your multiple is 5.

By crunching these numbers, you see that your EBITDA of $600,000 and your multiple of 5 result in a total valuation of $3 million. Since your goal is to sell the business for $5 million, you find that you're only $2 million short of your ideal valuation.

In this case, you should work to build up your revenue, manage your assets, and either keep your EBITDA in place or increase it. This way, you can realize your goal of $5 million, hit that goal, and sell your business.

Pro tip: if you can make improvements to the system of your business, there's a likelihood that the applicable multiple could be increased.

You should keep in mind, though... This approach is, in some ways, a gamble.

Consider the story of the body shop owner that we discussed earlier in this book. The body shop owner's business value was in dispute when he passed away. He waited to take these steps until much later in his life.

Of course, his situation is no one's fault - but this is a prime example showing the importance of planning as early on as possible.

Planning Ahead Can Give You The Best Chance Of Success

The best way to be truly successful in your estate planning efforts is to start when you have the most amount of time on your side - not when your circumstances have forced you to do it.

This is especially important when you consider the "Five D's of What-If Planning":

- Death
- Divorce
- Disability
- Disagreement
- Distress

Even before you plan to sell your business, you have to keep in mind that any "What If" could happen at any time.

What's more, creating a complete business plan takes time. From putting your entity documents in place to finding a valuation for your enterprise – the process can take anywhere from 12 to 18 months.

Though the timing of the process can be longer than you might think, your plan will be an incredible investment in saving the future value of all your efforts.

When No One Can "Take Over"

If no one is willing or able to take over your family business, you'll want to be particularly thoughtful about your business planning needs.

If you run a business that requires a particular skill or expertise, you may not be able to set up a plan for sale. However, there may be alternative options, including listing a family member as a supervisor, manager, or stockholder.

Additionally, in instances where there is trust, it is especially common for family members to sit on the company's board. As the board makes decisions regarding who would be the CEO and fill other essential roles in the company, that family member could participate and keep the business running through this role.

Selling And Staying Involved

If you find yourself asking, "Can I sell my business and stay involved? Is that a good idea?"

You're not alone. But whether or not this is the right decision for you will depend on a number of factors.

If you do choose to stay involved, the process usually looks like this . . .

The business will be sold to a larger entity or competitor. Once you've transferred the funds, you may be kept onboard for a period of time – anywhere from a few months to a few years. After this period has elapsed, you will typically be held to a non-compete agreement.

Whether the specifics of your sale agreement work in a similar way or not – and depending on your goals moving forward – you may choose to stay on, or you may choose to be done. Ultimately, the choice will be dependent on your circumstances and then left up to you.

CHAPTER 9

HOW TO AVOID THE PITFALLS OF BAD ESTATE PLANNING

Understanding what you should avoid when estate planning is just as important as knowing what you should look for. This way, you can be prepared for "what-ifs" - even before you get started making your plan.

What's In Your Plan?

The greatest pitfall that you can find in estate planning boils down to what plan did you actually buy? Did you buy your estate plan online? Do you have a one-size-fits-all plan from a lawyer offering plans at a discount? Or do you have a plan that is tailored to your specific goals?

A classic example of this can be found in an experience I had with a client a few years ago.

They had emigrated from Europe to the United States years before I met them. Since becoming American citizens, they accumulated approximately $5 million in assets. When they came to my office, they proudly told me that they each had a Will that only cost $600. This immediately triggered a red flag.

So I asked them, "Do you know what you bought with that?" And this gentleman, who was an experienced businessman during his professional life looked at me as if I had three heads.

He asked, "What do you mean what did I buy with that?"

I explained that with a $5 million estate, he bought a 9 to 14-month probate case that would probably cost a minimum of about $65,000 in attorney's fees. I left out the cost of the valuations for certain assets that were in it.

(By the way, property valuations can be relatively inexpensive – costing maybe $1,000 to $2,000 depending on the type of property. Business valuations, on the other hand, start at $15,000 and go up from there. If you have multiple businesses in your estate, these valuation costs begin snowballing.)

My client stared back at me with empty eyes. He was the deer in the headlights. The explanation of how a Will works and what the hidden costs could be completely surprised him. Most people don't like surprises, and he was no exception. His surprise quickly turned to frustration and anger.

The pitfall was that they didn't know what they were paying for when they bought their Will. They received a document, not a plan. This mistake can be easily avoided.

Prepare For Any Contingencies - Even The Unexpected Ones

Another classic pitfall lies in having a plan that doesn't really protect you from the "Five D's of What-If Planning": Death, Divorce, Disability, Disagreement, and Distress.

We'll use another example to illustrate this point.

Two young entrepreneurs visited my office for a consultation. They were starting a company, and they intended to do everything right.

They had a decent business plan, a good idea, and had identified their perfect client. So, I asked them what I would ask any business partner, "How are you going to own this company?"

Confidently, they replied, "Fifty-fifty." Well, up went the red flag in my mind.

Fifty-fifty is disastrous for business planning because there is no majority. In a fifty-fifty plan, you must ask what-ifs like, "What if you deadlock with one person saying yes and the other person saying no?"

They looked at each other, and then at me. They responded, "But, we agree on everything."

So I asked, "Well, what happens when you don't?"

They were firm, "No, no, no, we agree on everything." And no matter the "what-ifs" I presented, they stood firm on this point.

We ended the meeting only 10 minutes later. There was no way I could help them. There was always going to be a possibility of disagreement. Not only did they not have a solution for it, but they also wouldn't even have the discussion.

In every even-numbered business partnership, (whether it's two people, four people, etc.), there will always be some type of disagreement. The biggest pitfall these people face is that they haven't planned for what a disagreement looks like – or what to do when it happens.

This is crucial because these inevitable disagreements can mean the death of the business – especially if it's a small one.

Stay Away From "Ages and Stages"

In estate planning, there's a concept called "Ages and Stages". This is where, in a trust or a plan, you say that your assets go to the heirs in stages once they reach a certain age.

For example, you might say that your daughter will get 50% of her inheritance at age 25, then half of the remainder at age 35, and then the remaining balance at age 45.

Initially, this seems like good "what-if" planning. "What if my son has bad judgment when it comes to his choice of a spouse?" "What if he gets divorced and that spouse takes half of the family money?"

But, while these are good "what-ifs" to be planning for, Ages and Stages of planning leave your assets in danger. Why? Because it wipes out the protection that your heir has in their vested right to distribution.

The downside of Ages and Stages planning is that it creates an opportunity for a creditor to come in and take the next scheduled distribution.

Under an Ages and Stages plan, creditors won't be able to collect on the initial inheritance but when the next "Age and Stage" comes around, they can make a claim.

In Conclusion

You might characterize these points as not going far enough down the rabbit hole. Of course, we can sit and plan for potential contingencies as far as the eye can see. But while there's a reasonable amount of contingencies to plan for – at some point you have to just let it go.

Florida recently changed its laws to allow trusts to exist in the state for up to 1,000 years. But who can plan for 1,000 years ahead?

You can reasonably make a plan for two and three generations ahead, but you have to ask yourself, "What is the real benefit of these efforts?"

The most important thing is that you are planning ahead – and that you have an expert on your side who can help you decide when to keep going, and when you've done everything that you can.

CHAPTER 10

HOW I CAN HELP

After reading this book, I hope that you understand how important it is to protect your legacy. I also hope that you have a better understanding of how you might achieve that goal.

This work is incredibly important to me because I have seen firsthand how life can turn upside down in an instant. That's why I have dedicated my career to helping people just like you.

If you're looking for an attorney who can help you get on the road to a secure future, I'd be happy to talk with you and see what we might be able to do together.

Our Approach Is To Support You In Every Way We Can

At my firm, we plan comprehensively. We don't look at business planning and estate planning as separate concepts. We understand that these issues are a single concept. We know that the primary wealth in the estate of a business owner is their business.

Our goal is to allow you to focus on building your business and to keep doing what makes you successful. What's more, we want to help you realize the benefits of all your efforts during your lifetime.

We want you to see the benefits of planning, and we want to help you sleep soundly at night knowing that you have a strategy in place for when a "what if" may strike.

Whenever we can, we want to help you achieve a more advantageous tax position, so we'll work with your other advisors to maximize the growth of your assets.

What makes us different from other firms is that we know that you're more than your assets and your bank account.

We Can Help You Can Make A Plan That Protects Every Part Of Your Legacy

I have a client who's wildly successful. He built an international business without even so much as high school education.

Imagine what a disservice it would be to that client's family not to memorialize the experience, knowledge, and wisdom that this person gained from building a business around the world.

The client's children will never be able to adequately tell their grandchildren about what the person who created all this was like. How could you convey a story like this in a way that would do it justice?

We asked ourselves this question, and we found one more "what-if" – but this one was different from the others. It wasn't rooted in the crises that can happen but in the possibility of being able to create a gift that could last for generations.

That's when we came up with the idea for something priceless and long-lasting – Legacy Interviews.

If you build an estate plan with our firm, you'll have the opportunity to pass on something that's even more valuable than your wealth. . . you'll be able to pass on your story.

Over the course of your planning with us, we can help you create a series of interviews over time that record your experiences, your testimony, your life, and how you got to where you are today.

That's real asset value. That's wealth. The greatest gift that you can give to those you love isn't just money, it isn't just a business – it's the lessons that got you there.

There's an age-old phrase in the estate planning industry... "The first generation makes the money, the second generation manages the money, and the third generation loses the money."

It's a story that is told in family businesses time and time again. And yet, there's a small percentage of people that say "That's not going to be me."

Those people work with us.

CHAPTER 11

THE ART OF NEGOTIATION

We negotiate every single day.

In fact, every moment of every day, anytime we interact with somebody, it's probably a negotiation.

Lawyers have a horrible reputation for communication – in part because some use phrases like this: **GOVERN YOURSELF ACCORDINGLY.** This phrase is usually at the end of a letter that claims that you did something wrong and demands that you fix it immediately, or risk facing legal action against you.

If a letter like this lands on your desk, what do you do? For most people, their blood pressure rises and they get defensive. They'll say, "I'm going to fight this all the way to the Supreme Court. I'm never going to back down because it's the principle of the thing."

Then, people get entrenched on their respective sides. But, in many cases, the only thing that happens is that both sides end up contributing to their lawyer's retirement fund. That's it.

After 12 years as a commercial litigator, I learned that the court process doesn't necessarily solve everyone's problems. In many cases, it only drags these issues out because of the formalities related to rules, evidence, and procedures that govern what can be presented and when.

There's a reason why about 95% of lawsuits in this country settle rather than go to trial – because most people don't want to put their case in the hands of the jury. After all, who knows what the jury is going to do?

This means that, eventually, you'll have to negotiate.

To get this negotiation done, we've created formal structures like mediation. Unfortunately, many mediators act like novice diplomats going from one room to the other saying things like, "They're offering $100,000 and you want $200,000 so let's just meet in the middle at $150,000." Then everybody goes home miserable.

But is this really a negotiation? No.

People have different goals for negotiations. Some people want to maximize their dollar value, while some people are attempting to minimize risk. There are a number of things that come into negotiation. These issues shouldn't simply get reduced to finding the average of the two financial positions.

Negotiation is really about:

- Getting to the deeper issues
- Bringing those issues out into the open

- Addressing them from a position of empathy
- Working with what you have
- Then reaching an agreement

If we're really successful at negotiation, we get the other side to solve our problem for us – *but how do we get to those deeper issues without blowing up the deal?*

When it comes to business and estate planning, *how do we ensure that your heirs and family members negotiate rather than fight?*

When I think about negotiation as it pertains to this book, I have to ask myself, "How do I create an environment where, if there's a disagreement, my kids will negotiate with each other – rather than fight each other?"

The answer to this question is different for everyone, but it's one of those "what-ifs" that you can only address if you ask the question in the first place.

There's a science to negotiation that is mostly based on psychology, and then there's an art to negotiation. At my firm, we make it a point to be specially trained on this, because we've seen the impact that it has on our ability to resolve disputes across the board.

We focus on negotiation because it helps us to be prepared for every "what-if" that might ever come your way. We know that business owners don't want to "bet" their business and life savings on a court case that might have an uncertain outcome.

Instead, we make it our job to know the best tools to maximize success and mitigate any downside.

Negotiation does this because it can speed up the dispute resolution process, it can help everyone feel good at the end of the process, it's much more productive, it's faster, and it's more enjoyable.

INDEX

S

T

W

Notes

Made in the USA
Monee, IL
15 September 2026

63205752R00074